Bodies of Separation

Bodies of Separation
© Chim Sher Ting / Cathexis Northwest Press

No part of this book may be reproduced without written permission of the publisher or author, except in reviews and articles.

First Printing: 2023

Paperback ISBN: 978-1-952869-74-7

Cover Design by © YY Liak, 2022.
Editing & Interior Design by C. M. Tollefson

Cathexis Northwest Press

cathexisnorthwestpress.com

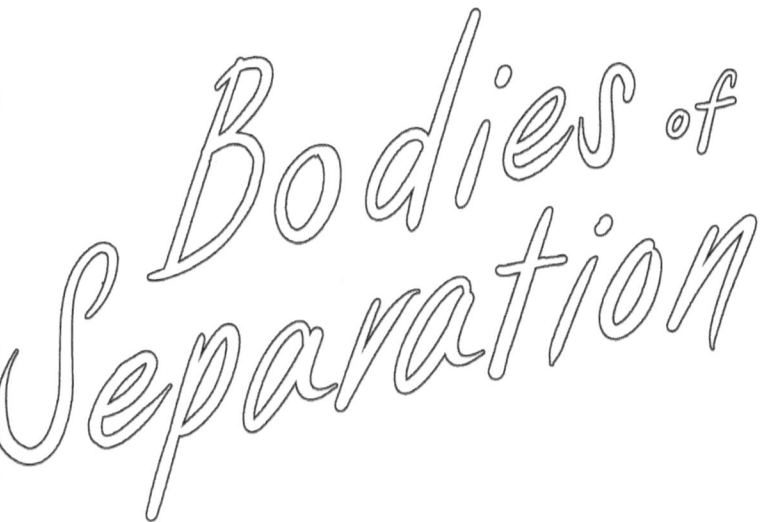

Bodies of Separation

CHIM SHER TING

Cathexis Northwest Press

To my family, whose love has transcended language and time

TABLE OF CONTENTS

一 (n.):	21
They Told Me A Dragon Was A Phoenix That Never Rose From Ashes	23
Ah Ma	24
Iconography Of A Thread[1]	25
Hunger	26
A Glossary of Unspoken Terms	27
How Every Bird Has Clipped Its Ancestry and Made Itself Into Something Lovable	29
Yellow Fever	30
The Things We Call Beautiful	31
渴望 (v.):	33
Water Dialectics	35
A Mudskipper's Love Song	36
This, An Approximation of Pain:	38
Wound	39
50%	41
If M[1] was Marriage and M[2] was Migration,	43
The Anatomy of Silence	45
Autopsy	46

CONTENT WARNINGS

Yellow Fever: War
This, An Approximation of Pain: War, corporal punishment
Autopsy: Death

⟶ (N.):

I languish beneath Warburton's night-sky,
untouched by light,

Learning how an expanse is another space
a body has shunned,

The body made to abandon / its space / a silence
my hesitation has come to fill,

Before gliding over
the fricatives of a name.

When I was 8 in a class
of white faces,

I spoke in hushed tones to sand
down the mountains of phonemes.

I expunged allophones to become
what was expected of me.

Before 慧田 became Winnie and
丽英 became Lily,

There was night, and a body that sought
white and christened it

A luminous flux.

I came to learn that our names were all expanse,
2718 miles and the length of an umbilical cord.

When I was 10, my teacher told me to
stop writing my name in alien letters

No one could understand. I didn't tell him

I once looked through
each character and saw the river home.

When I was 15, I bleached the womb
that had no memory of me.

I called this land home, a daughter
on her knees.

These days, I still drive on Eagle Highway,
stopping in the sand to call my old name

                                        to the moon.

The gibbous moon splits in half —

I make a wish, and pull it
till it snaps like charred bones.

THEY TOLD ME A DRAGON WAS A PHOENIX THAT NEVER ROSE FROM ASHES

Standing on the platform in Albury,
    thinking about dead carnations and chipped
    porcelain, thinking about gelid lakes
  and the ten years between us, diametrical distance,
my mother lamenting her prodigal daughter's accent
on the phone, thinking about telephone lines
and how some cords unravel
more quickly than others, about gibbous moons
    and how some shadows fasten
        to the countenance of another.
            There are some trees that bury
                their lineages beneath their skins,
        showing that even dragons can be forgotten.
    In Chinese, there is a saying
    泼出去的水，不可能拿回来。
    I'm standing on the platform, in the middle
  of January, trying to recall the name of a passing freight in
Chinese. In the legends, dragons
    rose from the sea but there were some
        made only for ruin.
            At the last flicker of a white-hot
                firecracker, I let the rhotic coda unfurl
            its tail and the four-tones of a *white language*
            vanishes beneath the waves.
        When the train rushes the platform,
    I think how some winters blow
more maelstrom than others
        and even though we've thought little of history
        how little we have perceived of death.

AH MA

What is distance
but the aubade

of an ocean—: a body—:
a mother tongue?

I watched you unclench
your jaw, dragging morphemes

across the ocean,
to teach me the difference

between ná and nà.

How I recoiled from
     each
           inflection
               like
                     the
                                 barrel
                          of
               a
     gun,

where each word
was crushed

like a blossom
in my hand.

How you shuddered
each diphthong,

watching your only grandchild
drift cordless from the motherland.

At the epicenter
of your chest,

Failure—:

the size of
a gunshot wound.

ICONOGRAPHY OF A THREAD[1]

归： This is me lying with my back
away from you,
as you reached for my hand.

心： The rain falling
all around us
like our failures

And I think back
to simpler times

似： When you carried me on your back,
walking stick in hand,

箭： And we crawled over
the strawberry fields,

Over
the moon,

And into
the hook

Of an eye

---

[1] 归心似箭 means a heart that longs to return home as swiftly as the flight of an arrow

HUNGER

饭[2] and 烦[3]

Funny how two words phoneticised the same in Chinese
but meant vastly different things.

How 饭 was the ivory harvest from
fields of salt and rain,

ploughed to fruition through
thunderclouds and a wrist of light.

How 烦 was the keening of a storm,
the frustration of a sky at the weight of its libations.

Maybe that was what I was—wild rice,
the amalgamation of two entities,

growing with increasing frustration at a body
with too little love for me,

opening my hips the width of the sky,
waiting for the birth of a harvest.

---

[2] fàn
[3] fán

A GLOSSARY OF UNSPOKEN TERMS

怀孕／运 : Some people have never known lucky, and that's how they learn forgiveness. My mother said we had many people we had to forgive. But I grew up in an attap house, amidst salt and wild paddy, chasing mudskippers and balking at thunder with fistfuls of rain. I never thought that was anything other than lucky.

变化 : They moved us into a high-rise apartment and told us change was good. Even then, I knew good was a nebulous, understated idea constantly shifting within the four walls of chipped mortar and molted cigars. When we left, the mudskippers had run into the *longkang* and drowned. The ones that survived learnt to climb trees in school uniforms, their shirt tails flapping in the wind like a flag of surrender.

影子 : My mother's shadow, like the long ear of the moon, follows me. *Sit up straight.* An accent that sounded smooth like butter on the television, now feels clunky and precarious on my tongue. I ate baos for a week to save up enough for a designer bag from the mall basement, just like those I'd seen on Pretty Woman. My mother asks, *why are you rocking a boat that has been safe all this while?* But maybe this was my coming-of-age ritual, a test I had to pass to become all that I was meant to be, like the 5 o-clock shadow of a boy.

刻苦 : There are some things that stay with you. For me, the first time someone laughed at the hole in my shoes. The first time someone told me they gave my mother a quarter at the local laundromat. I imagined running a knife through marrow to find 6-year old you with 20-pence, alone on a stoop, staring at a bun-cart just 5-pence short while your mother works the graveyard shift as a go-go dancer. 9-year old you running barefoot to school through rain and torrential mud as you wear through your last good pair of shoes, all the while your parents are smoking and dancing through the final chorus of 何日君再来.

自怨／愿: Some people have lived all their lives for worse. And if they lived long enough, it became even the best part of them.

反映 : So then, does it make me the bad person for leaving, or does it make you one for only having the courage to stay? Or maybe, good and evil are merely a false dichotomy to detract from the larger burden of our lives? As if any choice was solely our own. Maybe this was why I hated painting, even as a child— how every dot would bleed into another until the whole sheet was ruined. How every dot of your life has bled into another to leave you crying into the fishbowl-eye of a laundry machine.

离别 : Leaving for a better place? Hope? Idea? Maybe a better ending.

小谎 : Do you know there is no direct translation for a white lie in Chinese? They call it a small lie, a lie of kindness. But there was nothing small or kind about what I'd said, which was *I'll come back   I swear, I'll come back.*

麻辣 : When all the pain was done and felt, there was only indifference from a thorn that should have been uprooted many years ago.

渴望 : For every person that walks away, there is a mother, looking out the window, calling after them to stay. *Stay.*

HOW EVERY BIRD HAS CLIPPED ITS ANCESTRY AND MADE ITSELF INTO SOMETHING LOVABLE

The swallows are leaving home for the summer. The trail of wings unspooling a thread of questions to their former nest: How are you doing? Have you been well?

Solitude is every answer denied a table, a heart closing into a fist.

Distance exposes the strangers in our conversation. How you make the habit of thumping your chest three times to clear the wetness in your throat before you speak. How you skim words like a pebble skinning an ocean. Since young, I had liked writing 飞 as 飛, believing that 飛 was a rising phoenix till it had its wings clipped that made it a singular boring entity 飞.

You tell me Aunt Lee's son graduated college, how Auntie Joan left her keys at the laundromat again. Useless facts make you feel important somehow. Give you a reason to call. Like we are age 13, sifting sand in the backyard to exhume gold. Age 30, trying to recall that one song we were arguing to that one time on the radio when travelling to Disneyland. Because every truth was a thing unspoken, every unspoken thing was our own four-letter word. When I said "Shit, I love you", you told me not to say that word, and I asked you which one?

Naked telephone lines, brittle cords. How easily they break under the weight of our pauses. Yet, in the maddening silence, even the last bird of the flock looks back when he leaves. Just as even a hatchling recognises the face of its mother, I come back to you. In my mind, sometimes.

Under the splintering clouds, the sky brilliant as a thimble, I thump my chest three times and hope that somewhere, you're doing the same.

YELLOW FEVER

> 希望 *(xī wàng)(n.): Hope. See also:* 息望 *(xī wàng) (to extinguish all hope).*
> *Or* 西望 *(xī wàng), to look to the West.*

But what does it mean to be saved? You
with your thumb on my jugular, learning
the crest of my breath, telling me
you were made for destruction but tonight,
tonight, we will build cities from the bones you've made.
Tell me, blue-eyed lover, wisdom wielder from whom
all answers were born, why is it when someone
says superhero, my mind only comes up white?
How you'd mouth through and break
the womb of another country to satisfy your desire.
In the back of a faded green Camry, five past
midnight on the dime of a gasoline, your grandfather
once reached for the arms of another
country and called it mercy. When she broke—
all river, seed and bloodied thread—he christened
her indecent. Years later, he'd sit at the bar, dusting
the napalm out of his hair, laughing about that
one encounter he had with the mysterious woman
from a land he couldn't pronounce. Oriental princess.
China doll. The names of your fantasy
sound like a sullied myth. Rain
phosphorescing backwards,
falling through the eye
into every good part
till it has renounced an ancestral wound.
Our rabbits lie, moon-orphaned and unmarked
in their graves. You press a thumbprint
into my back, some victim of causality, to mark
the hour I'd learn about all the other legends
our grandmothers foretold.
So then, what does it mean to be saved?
I've had faith in dragons lesser than you.

THE THINGS WE CALL BEAUTIFUL

Inspired by the Good Characters Chinese Alphabet

When I was in sixth grade, my teacher told me
to transliterate my name into Chinese characters.

She tells me Chinese is a beautiful *Orient* language,
and how lucky I am to be Chinese.

So I wrote: 弓升三尺　　七工内巨

Bow rises three feet
Seven labours inside giants.

It means nothing to me.

That day, I returned home and flushed
my assignment down the toilet.

How it choked, water spilling ov-
er the curve of porcelain, and I thought:

Should I have made a mess, if only
to be seen?

My mother kneads balm like cattle brand
onto her wrists from the mornings spent
slicing fishgut.

She shouts a mandarin dialect
across the market floor like a soldier
heading out for war, and

My grandfather walks out
an old cab accident with metal
in his back.

Every month, my mother brings me
to the wishing tree and whispers
my name eight times for luck.

I tell her my teacher doesn't know
I was named for snow on the pavilion,
powdered wisteria on slate-grey beams,

She tells me
no one ever does.

In animal chess, my grandma always
chooses the rat and sends it
north of the river.

When water spills over its ankles,
everyone marvels
at the exquisiteness of its survival.

And she tells me how beautiful is
the rat that consumes an elephant
when the world is looking away.

渴望 (V.):

Every day, my mother calls
and asks if I'm okay,

When what she really means is:
How's the weather?

And I want to tell her
it is 20 degrees and feels

Like something is about to die.

Last weekend, someone broke
into the local Asian grocer's, wrote

GO BACK TO YOUR COUNTRY in red
block letters across the window.

The owner arrived
the next morning,

Swept up the glass shards, and
reopened the store for the day.

Last weekend, my friends and I
watched Karate Kid,

And they told me to raise
my fists in a *flying tiger-dragon stance*.

They taunted,
Show us some kung fu.

Like come on, *make yourself into
something interesting.*

They said, what doesn't kill you
makes you stronger, but

Why does our existence
have to be a fight?

The sun rises with the
pounding of pestle on mortar,

Bleeds what burns from the skins
of peppercorn and star anise.

My skin silvers
from bare-knuckling

What has always
been cold to touch—

The corpses in another headline,
the silence that follows

When you say *Asia is not as poor
as you think it is.*

When my mother calls,
I say that I'm okay,

When what I really want to say is:

Ma, the sun is the same
here as it is back in our country.

When it rains,
it's a flood even God ignores.

Yesterday, someone called
out *these f--- Chinese* on the street and

I began running.

They said yellow, and I knew
they meant *jaundiced*,

Not sun-spangled,
not starry-eyed.

I ran till, all around me,
it was blue like the sky, and

I wondered if enough ocean
passes through me,

Would I become
luminous too?

Would I become a colour that
even I could die to love?

WATER DIALECTICS

O rain, and how little it cares
about the bodies it ruins.

O river, and how swiftly it flows
from its place of origin.

And I've always wondered how could we
crave the ocean this much?

When all around us is water,

When all around us, we've been
sinking like a stone.

A MUDSKIPPER'S LOVE SONG

The radio had stopped singing
康定情歌 by A-Mei
as you picked a string of yarn
through the eye of the needle, humming

                a ditty about mudskippers
                and landslides
                neither of us could name.

When you said, *ah girl, this is progress,*
or this house would be buried beneath
mud and rain, the same way you'd say
don't look that white man in the eye or
don't place your fingers near the stove,

                I cranked up the knob on the radio static,
                which sounded like the
                steady drum of distant hooves.

Progress was the fact that I'm not dead or dying.

You told me you learnt a new word
today on the train to work -
                              S H I T.

      S-H-I-T.

                                  HE SAID: Y O U. S H I T.
     屎?

                        是的。

Like mud and rain.

You sat in front of the radio all night,
learning the English words for
how are you and have a nice day
so no one would scold you again,

                all the while humming
                about mudskippers and
                pouring rain.

Ah girl, this is progress,
when I can sing about mudslides,
knowing it wouldn't happen to me.

> I watched you repeat the words over and
> over, your mouth curling the shape of an
> R, till you had dug a valley beneath your
> feet.

> Away from the scree of allotones
> and rhotic codas circling the summer air.

I told you you should learn some words
for yourself.

Something else
besides good and fine.

> You said they were all you needed to
> know—

But Ah Ma,
weeds grow where everything is "fine'.

> I read yesterday, that even those
> mudskippers you love die when
> they're submerged in
> unadulterated salt.

THIS, AN APPROXIMATION OF PAIN:

The long rod, made of horse-whip and
                white lightning, cracking violent static
as it curved through the air. The lashes on the back,
                counting *I love you* on a D flat minor scale
I had wrestled the night to learn, crying we
                all want something we can't have.
That golden child opening doors
                across a suburban sky. That sky folding
into lullabies beneath our skin.
                When you darkened your face with ash
from the pipes, sank beneath the gap
                between the floorboards to the sound of
AK-47s splitting the air, you told yourself
                this was not the life you wanted.
When you survived a sky lampooned with
                silvered blisters and orange fires
to be denied school, you hoped that the apple should
                fall further from the tree.
The tree: a wilted hollow, excavating prayers
                from the trabeculous rattle of loved ones.
Her apple, bloated from epicanthal salt,
                drifts aimless on a harbour of ghosts.
I'm tired of these white-marbled
                graves for our language of love.
How we made weak humour from unfinished pain :
                Exhausting the metaphor of a tiger parent :
Injecting memories like napalm
                through the veins. You cracked the cane
and saw the faces of the men who stormed
                your home — the knife, a pillar of salt,
in your hand. When the last note echoed through
                our porcelain home, the bamboo rod rippled
like lightning or the whistle of the bullet
                of a soldier rushing the pews of a church,
and you made a soldier
                the only way you knew how.

WOUND

This is the flag wound
around my finger.

The man across the table
tells me to break my name
in three places across the dotted lines.

He tells me to hold
my hand over my chest
like a sinner rewriting a crime,

Tells me to commit
these clauses to memory
like rivets through the hands.

Somewhere across town,
a man stands across the yard
with a picket sign, yelling

We don't sing songs about orphans here.

The white sting of a blue sky
and golden classic like napalm
through the veins.

Khe Sanh.

O, to hear the anthem of another gun
against the temple of my people,

The white rifle through
the streets of Hong Kong.

Hear the barrel open
through the skull of a fallen soldier

Into a love profaned and deserted
on the bed of an *Oriental Princess.*

Against a sky shot through
with desire,

A man on the street ties a string
around my wrist

And asks me
to buy my freedom:

He tells me there is a price for everything.

Bones line the tarmac between
my country, this house and the ocean.

My mother tells me
to avoid looking at the trees.

*But Ma, there are some things in this world
far scarier than ghosts.*

I still hear the sound of my ancestral
tablet breaking into three,

The wild thunder of my great-
grandmother's voice rising like an anvil.

Somewhere, a cord unravels
like a foreign tongue.

My mother's cry, like
a stranger's kiss,

Follows me
everywhere.

50%

I once thought the Australia Cup was something
you could drink.

I ate my porridge with vegemite,
consumed Tim Tams on New Year's Eve.

Rubbed Zam-Buk on my calves
and called mosquitoes "mozzies".

Went online to get a cheongsam
but bought a peony imprint instead.

In this land, where the sun was an oleograph behind
a mahogany desk and an oath,

They told me the flags only flew at half-mast
to salute the dead.

That bodies, at half-mast,
were broken like a vow.

At City Hall, the day I submitted my documents,
they performed open heart surgery.

Sevofluorane, propofol,
morphine:

These were the things
needed to silence a person.

They knifed open my heart and found
half a biloba tree living through saltwater.

Followed a vessel and found it
circling a white meniscus lunatus.

The blue light inscribed on the calyces
of my bones.

And I asked them how much
should I have to bleed to be considered adequate —

                30%? 50%?

They told me till I flat-lined—
and there, we can start over.

IF M_1 WAS MARRIAGE AND M_2 WAS MIGRATION,

then $M_1 - M_2$ = the vows we made from 0.

When I changed my name
from diphthongs to the platonic

symmetry of deep tongues,
I realised all love was a mistake.

  1
+ 1,
an unequal possession.

The act of one body seeking
ownership over another.

The act of a body abnegating at the transept
with a desire to be christened

integral. Before there was motion,
there was a game we played, where I

named our roots and my mother pretended
they didn't exist. To last forever, my mother said,

you took the thing you lov-
                ed and you divided it

till it meant nothing. You took the fractals of your love
    and made it the fraction of a whole.

All this white space

was just an asymptote, rising
into oblivion like a lie,

where y was the sky
   and x was the reciprocal of our parts.

She said, marriage + migration = two points on the same plane.

We stood on one plot
with a stake through our hearts

and where it ended,
person or land,

there was freedom only
in what remained untouched.

THE ANATOMY OF SILENCE

吞

These are the peonies of a dialect
blooming up through

The snow, a thinning white lipstick
on the by-road,

These are the elderberries like clots
of blood on alabaster,

They surround a tongue of alder trees
like a discarded love-knot,

The vineyard, silvered twine around
marbled valleculae.

Whispering morphemes as proof
of an inheritance.

They burnish sickle into stele
like reaping crozier through a tooth,

人

Pulling synapses
from those they'd left behind.

This is the belling of wind through
a mouth of open foliage,

二

Two stock-thin persimmons
colliding as a dyad.

These are the stippling papers
loosing like cartilage into

The blackbird,
a stranger to plum blossoms,

the bog, ribbons of prayers stretching
the length of a larynx,

Rises into vocative air,

口

an accent,

They reach their plumage into the
mildew-sun
like candles searching for a wick,

And swallows
the native sound.

And softly,
in an act of malaise-

-Ah, they collapse upon
the last of the light.

AUTOPSY

I once autopsied
a man who left his country.

Thinking I'd find bones,
milk-white and carved in another language.

Thinking I'd find vessels,
strung through the blood of rebellion.

But I found a heart emptied of ocean
忍,
from when he held knife to myocardium.

When they asked him to repeat his name
all over again,
(all over again)
like he's a wind-up monkey, rounding out clanging cymbals to
effusive applause
and he wants to cry but he's dehydrated, so
he says he's run out of breath.

When water leaves, it always finds first
the silent cavity of the lungs.

Did you know a person lasts 3 minutes under-
water, in his utopia of silence,
before he finally drowns?

The wound was always
a WHY through the chest,

From nipple-line to gut,
so it's quickest to get to the heart.

But the answer was always a wound
stitched backwards,

A mouth sealing itself
shut.

They said bodies stiffen in the face of fear
but have they seen rigor mortis,

When all myofibrils are pointed
the direction home?

When the paramedics pulled him out
after all the time spent underwater,

They thought he'd survive,

But his skin had been stripped, and
he'd lost the ability to speak.

He choked on air and
passed all the same,

His mouth purpling
the shade of a vow.

Thank you to the wonderful poets I've worked with, who have provided feedback on these poems, that they may become what they are today: Elena Gomez, Mary-Jean Chan and Afshan D'souza-Lodhi.

Thank you to the following journals who have allowed me to grace their pages with earlier versions of these poems: ⎯ (n.) in OSU The Journal, They Told Me A Dragon Was A Phoenix That Never Rose From Ashes in Salamander, Yellow Fever in Pleiades, Wound in Tahoma Literary Review, The Things We Call Beautiful in The Pinch, Ah Ma in Rust and Moth, A Mudskipper's Love Song in North Dakota Quarterly, This, An Approximation of Pain in Chestnut Review, How Every Bird Has Clipped Its Ancestry and Made Itself Into Something Lovable (previously published as The Flight of Swallows) in FlashFlood Journal as part of National Flash Fiction Day, A Glossary of Unspoken Terms in TIMBER Journal, and Hunger in The Citron Review.

Thank you to my family, Dexter, Celine and Ler Ting, for their ardent support for my poetry and for their constant encouragement to pursue my passion for language.

Thank you to my Ah Ma, Lee Pheck Eng, for showing me that, sometimes, love escapes even the best of our words.

Thank you to you, my reader, for journeying with me through these poems.

Originally from a sunny tropical island in Southeast Asia, Sher Ting is a Singaporean-Chinese currently residing in Australia. She is a 2021 Pushcart and Best of The Net nominee, in addition to being a 2021 Writeability Fellow with Writers Victoria and a finalist in The New York Times Asia-Pacific Writing Competition. She has work published in OSU The Journal, Pleiades, The Pinch, Rust and Moth and elsewhere. Her work speaks of themes of dislocation/dissociation, loneliness/loss and memory/nostalgia. She hopes, through her work, to highlight oft-rejected narratives of minority identity, in addition to exploring the plurality of the body and identity. She can be found at sherting.carrd.co

Also Available from Cathexis Northwest Press:

<u>Something To Cry About</u>
by Robert Krantz

<u>Suburban Hermeneutics</u>
by Ian Cappelli

<u>God's Love Is Very Busy</u>
by David Seung

<u>that one time we were almost people</u>
by Christian Czaniecki

<u>Fever Dream/Take Heart</u>
by Valyntina Grenier

<u>The Book of Night & Waking</u>
by Clif Mason

<u>Dead Birds of New Zealand</u>
by Christian Czaniecki

<u>The Weathering of Igneous Rockforms in High-Altitude Riparian Environments</u>
by John Belk

<u>If A Fish</u>
by George Burns

<u>How to Draw a Blank</u>
by Collin Van Son

<u>En Route</u>
by Jesse Wolfe

<u>sky bright psalms</u>
by Temple Cone

<u>Moonbird</u>
by Henry G. Stanton

<u>southern athiest. oh, honey</u>
by d. e. fulford

<u>Bruises, Birthmarks & Other Calamities</u>
by Nadine Klassen

<u>Wanted: Comedy, Addicts</u>
by AR Dugan

<u>They Curve Like Snakes</u>
by David Alexander McFarland

<u>the catalog of daily fears</u>
by Beth Dufford

<u>Shops Close Too Early</u>
by Josh Feit

<u>Vanity Unfair and Other Poems</u>
by Robert Eugene Rubino

<u>Destructive Heresies</u>
by Milo E. Gorgevska

<u>About Time</u>
by Julie Benesh

<u>The Night with James Dean</u>
by A.A. deFreese

Cathexis Northwest Press

www.ingramcontent.com/pod-product-compliance
Lightning Source LLC
Chambersburg PA
CBHW030139100526
44592CB00011B/962